31 Days of Declarations for Children

with Application and Journal

By Modupe Olakunle-Olabode

September 2021

FIRST EDITION

Cover by Joseph Bell
Edited by Meghan Bell

To God Almighty who inspired me to write this book.
It is a privilege.

Acknowledgments

I would like to give special thanks to all of the parents that have given me the opportunity to be a mother to their children while I wait for mine. And a special shout out to Ayomide and Nifemi Familola who are wonderful children to me. They are so special to me and I love them dearly.

Thank you to my husband, Olakunle, who is always there for me. I love you.

Introduction

To Parents and Guardians,
The Bible instructs parents to 'train a child how to live the right way, then even when he is old, he will still live that way' (Proverbs 22:5 ICB). The Word of God in the Bible teaches our children how to thrive in life and what to do in different situations. The aim of this book is to help you, as parents and carers, to study the word of God with your children every day. The fun part of it is that you grow together with your kids!

To Children,
When you go to school, you are taught how to read and write. But it's the Word of God in the Bible that teaches you how to love, how to forgive, how to behave well, how to respect others and much more. So it's important you read the Bible every day. With this book, you will learn how to read a verse from the Bible each day and practise what you read. You can use this as a journal and write down your thoughts every day. This will help you to memorise the verses. Go through this book with your grown up and have some fun!

Day 1

Declaration: I know who I am, I am a child of God.

Application: God will look after me today.

The Father has loved us so much! He loved us so much that we are called children of God. (1 John 3:1 ICB)

Day 1 Journal

Write down your thoughts about today's topic:

Day 2

Declaration: I am loved by God and I love God.

Application: God will protect me today.

The Lord appeared to us in the past, saying: "I have loved you with an everlasting I have drawn you with unfailing kindness. (Jeremiah 31:3 NKJV)

Day 2 Journal

Write down your thoughts about today's topic:

Day 3

Declaration: I am accepted by God.

Application: There is nothing Satan can do about it.

To the praise of the glory of His grace, by which He made us accepted in the Beloved. (Ephesians 1:6 NKJV)

Day 3 Journal

Write down your thoughts about today's topic:

Day 4

Declaration: I am forgiven.

Application: Sin has no power over me.

I write to you, dear children, because your sins are forgiven through Christ. (1John 2:12 ICB)

Day 4 Journal

Write down your thoughts about today's topic:

Day 5

Declaration: I am a victor.

Application: I am a winner today.

But in all these things we have full victory through God who showed his love for us. (Romans 8:37 ICB)

Day 5 Journal

Write down your thoughts about today's topic:

Day 6

Declaration: I am kind.

Application: I look for good in people today.

Be kind and compassionate to one another, forgiving each other, just as in Christ God forgave you.
(Ephesians 4:32 NIV)

Day 6 Journal

Write down your thoughts about today's topic:

Day 7

Declaration: I am a respectful person.

Application: I appreciate people in my life today.

Show respect for everyone. Love Christians everywhere. Fear God and honor the government. (1 Peter 2:17 LB)

Day 7 Journal

Write down your thoughts about today's topic:

Day 8

Declaration: I am beautiful in God's eyes.

Application: I reflect the glory of God today.

You are altogether beautiful, my darling there is no flaw in you. (Song of Solomon 4:7 NIV)

Day 8 Journal

Write down your thoughts about today's topic:

Day 9

Declaration: I am clever.

Application: I know what to do today by God's grace.

For I am Wisdom, and I am shrewd and intelligent. I have at my disposal living-understanding to devise a plan for your life. (Proverbs 8:12 TPT)

Day 9 Journal

Write down your thoughts about today's topic:

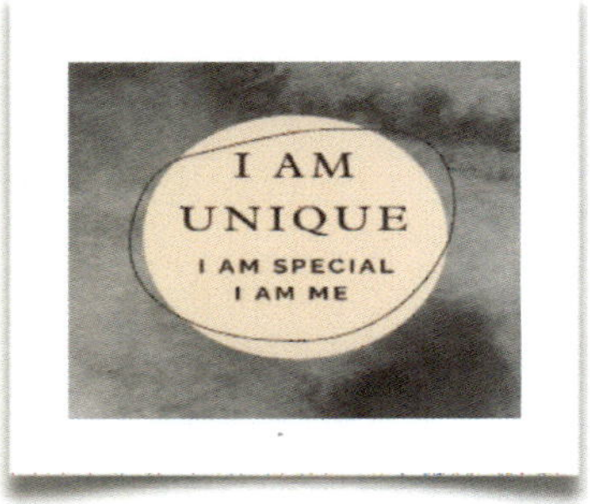

Day 10

Declaration: I am unique.

Application: I will not compare myself with other people.

Before I made you in your mother's womb, I chose you. Before you were born, I set you apart for a special work. I appointed you as a prophet to the nations. (Jeremiah 1:5 ICB)

Day 10 Journal

Write down your thoughts about today's topic:

Day 11

Declaration: I am wise.

Application: I will make good decision today with God's help.

But you have an anointing from the Holy One, and you know all things. (1John 2:20 NKJV)

Day 11 Journal

Write down your thoughts about today's topic:

Day 12

Declaration: I am highly favoured.

Application: I am surrounded by God's love and protection today.

For You, O Lord, will bless the righteous with favor You will surround him as with a shield. (Psalm 5:12 NKJV)

Day 12 Journal

Write down your thoughts about today's topic:

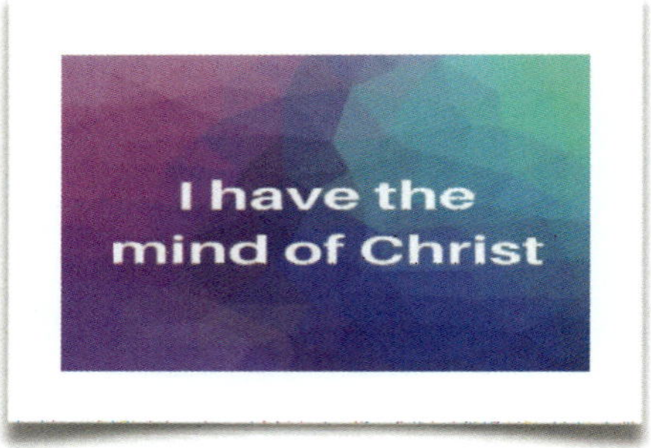

Day 13

Declaration: I have the mind of Christ.

Application: I think correctly today, and I will not be confused.

For "Who has known the mind of the Lord that he may instruct Him?" But we have the mind of Christ.
(1 Corinthians 2:16 NKJV)

Day 13 Journal

Write down your thoughts about today's topic:

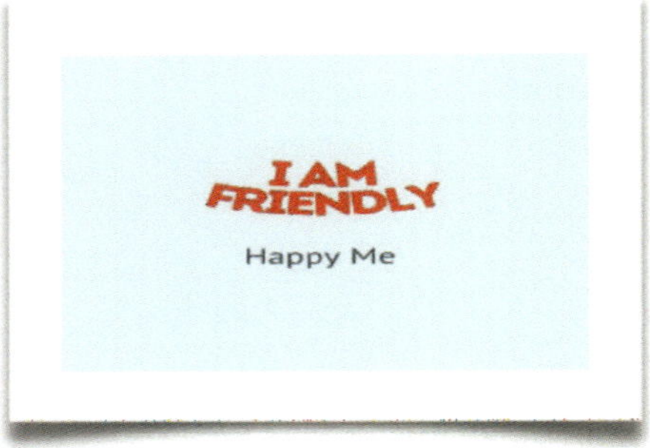

Day 14

Declaration: I am friendly.

Application: I am loving toward my friends and family today.

A friend loves you all the time. A brother is always there to help you. (Proverbs 17:17 ICB)

Day 14 Journal

Write down your thoughts about today's topic:

Day 15

Declaration: I am prayerful.

Application: I talk and listen to God throughout today.

Then He spoke a parable to them, that men always ought to pray and not lose heart. (Luke 18:1 NKJV)

Day 15 Journal

Write down your thoughts about today's topic:

Day 16

Declaration: I am generous.

Application: I enjoy helping my friends and family today.

It is good to be kind and generous. (Psalm 112:5 ICB)

Day 16 Journal

Write down your thoughts about today's topic:

Day 17

Declaration: I am bold.

Application: I know God is with me so I will not be afraid.

God did not give us a spirit that makes us afraid. He gave us a spirit of power and love and self-control.
(2 Timothy 1:7 ICB)

Day 17 Journal

Write down your thoughts about today's topic:

Day 18

Declaration: I love people.

Application: I will express my sincere love to someone today.

Most importantly, love each other deeply. Love has a way of not looking at others' sins. (1 Peter 4:8 ICB)

Day 18 Journal

Write down your thoughts about today's topic:

Day 19

Declaration: I am patient with myself and people.

Application: I will be calm if I do not get my way today.

Whoever is patient has great understanding, but one who is quick-tempered displays folly. (Proverbs 14:29 NIV)

Day 19 Journal

Write down your thoughts about today's topic:

Day 20

Declaration: I am a peaceful person.

Application: I am calm, friendly, and fearless today.

Try to live in peace with all people. And try to live lives free from sin. If anyone's life is not holy, he will never see the Lord. (Hebrews 12:14 ICB)

Day 20 Journal

Write down your thoughts about today's topic:

Day 21

Declaration: I am faithful.

Application: I will not lie today because I love God.

A faithful man will abound with blessings, but he who hastens to be rich will not go unpunished. (Proverbs 28:20 NKJV)

Day 21 Journal

Write down your thoughts about today's topic:

Day 22

Declaration: I am gentle with myself and people.

Application: I will not be too hard on myself and people.

No, your beauty should come from within you—the beauty of a gentle and quiet spirit. This beauty will never disappear, and it is worth very much to God. (1 Peter 3:4 ICB)

Day 22 Journal

Write down your thoughts about today's topic:

Day 23

Declaration: I am merciful.

Application: I will forgive others quickly today.

Those who give mercy to others are happy. Mercy will be given to them. (Matthew 5:7 ICB)

Day 23 Journal

Write down your thoughts about today's topic:

Day 24

Declaration: I am humble.

Application: I put others' interest before mine today.

For the Lord takes delight in his people he crowns the humble with victory. (Psalm 149:4 NIV)

Day 24 Journal

Write down your thoughts about today's topic:

Day 25

Declaration: I am full of joy.

Application: I will rejoice in the Lord no matter what happens today.

Give out a shout of cheer; sing for joy, O people of Zion, for great and mighty is the Holy One of Israel who lives among you. (Isaiah 12:6 TPT)

Day 25 Journal

Write down your thoughts about today's topic:

Day 26

Declaration: I am hopeful in God.

Application: There is no fear in me because I hope in God.

May the God of hope fill you with all joy and peace as you trust in him, so that you may overflow with hope by the power of the Holy Spirit. (Romans 15:13 NIV)

Day 26 Journal

Write down your thoughts about today's topic:

Day 27

Declaration: I am a grateful person.

Application: I thank God for my family and friends today.

Always give thanks to Father God for every person he brings into your life in the name of our Lord Jesus Christ.
(Ephesians 5:20 TPT)

Day 27 Journal

Write down your thoughts about today's topic:

Day 28

Declaration: I am comfortable with what I have.

Application: I am grateful to God for all that I have now.

Keep your lives free from the love of money. And be satisfied with what you have. God has said, "I will never leave you; I will never abandon you." (Hebrews 13:5 ICB)

Day 28 Journal

Write down your thoughts about today's topic:

Day 29

Declaration: I am gracious.

Application: I give thought to words before I say them.

Let your speech always be gracious, seasoned with salt, so that you may know how you ought to answer each person. (Colossians 4:6 ESV)

Day 29 Journal

Write down your thoughts about today's topic:

Day 30

Declaration: I have eternal life.

Application: I live my life through Jesus who lives in me.

I write this letter to you who believe in the Son of God. I write so that you will know that you have eternal life now. (1 John 5:13 ICB)

Day 30 Journal

Write down your thoughts about today's topic:

Day 31

Declaration: I am a winner.

Application: I will not quit trying until I win.

For everyone who has been born of God overcomes the world. And this is the victory that has overcome the world—our faith. (1 John 5:4 ESV)

Day 31 Journal

Write down your thoughts about today's topic:

Printed in Great Britain
by Amazon

67354137R00037